WASPS AT HOME

TEXT AND PHOTOGRAPHS BY
BIANCA LAVIES

DUTTON CHILDREN'S BOOKS
NEW YORK

This swirly gray nest, about two feet long, is home to a group of insects, a colony of wasps. They built it inside the wall of a house, out of paper that they made themselves. When the wall was ripped open for repair, part of the nest's outer covering was torn away too. Soon the wasps will repair the hole. But in the meantime, it is a window into their world. You can see them crawling around among the many little rooms, or cells, they built on different levels.

Yet much that goes on inside the nest you cannot see.

It is a world of darkness, vibrations, and chemical signals
that are hidden from human senses.

Many insects, including most wasps, live alone. They
hatch and grow up alone. They seek shelter and find food
alone. But the wasps in this nest live and work together,
helping one another. They are social wasps. They solve all
the problems that any individual animal must solve, but
they do this as a team.

There are many different kinds, or species, of social
wasps. The ones shown here are called yellowjackets.

Different kinds of social wasps build different sorts of nests. Some nests may be as small as Ping-Pong balls and others as large as basketballs. Some may be nestled close to the ground in grass or low bushes, while others may hang forty or fifty feet up in trees or against houses, barns, and other buildings.

Baldfaced hornets are a kind of social wasp. They built the nest shown below, about the size of a football, against a bathroom window. Beneath the papery layers of the nest's outer sheath, the hornets are busy at their tasks.

Although social wasps normally do not sting people unless pressed or squeezed, they do sting to defend their nests against intruders. Birds, rodents, coyotes, or bears sometimes bother a nest, looking to eat the wasp young inside. The stings of even a dozen angry wasps won't hurt a large animal protected by thick fur, but stings can be dangerous to a bird or small rodent—or to a person who has mistakenly upset a nest. The bathroom window remained shut while this nest was there.

These paper wasps, another kind of social wasp, built their nest against a porch ceiling. Paper wasp nests are always small—only one layer of cells, one comb. Because these wasps do not cover the comb with a sheath, it is easy to observe them. Filled with activity, a social wasp nest can be considered a lively family or colony. And that colony has one especially important goal—to produce wasp queens and their mates by summer's end.

Without wasp queens there would be no wasps or wasp nests. Queens are the only wasps that can mate with males. They are the only wasps that can start new nests by laying eggs that will produce more worker wasps, queens, and males. A queen is the mother in the nest. Her colony is her family. She creates it to ensure her own reproduction.

This yellowjacket queen has hidden herself in a woodpile, away from winter's wind and wet. There she will rest, neither moving nor eating, barely breathing, until warm spring days awaken her. Then she will fly off in search of a sugary food to give her energy—flower nectar or tree sap, perhaps. She'll find water, too. After that she will seek out a good place for her nest.

The paper wasp queen at left has chosen a sheltered corner of a porch ceiling for her nest. To make the paper, she found some weathered wood—a fence post or the side of an old house, most likely—and scraped off tiny splinters with her mouth. She softened them with water stored in her body, then chewed the splinters into a pulpy, papier-mâché-like ball.

Back at her nest site, she chewed the ball again, until the papery material was easy to spread. She attached a few dabs of pulp to the ceiling and drew them into a thin, tough stem that would support the whole nest. Then she began to fashion a few cells with her mouth, stopping to lay a tiny, pearly egg in each.

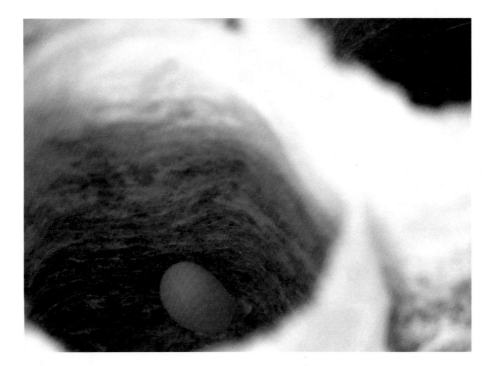

As the eggs travel down inside her body on their way to being laid, she fertilizes each with a drop of sperm. (Last fall, about eight months ago, she mated with several males and stored their sperm.) Finally, as each egg leaves her body, she coats it with a sticky substance, so it won't fall out of its cell. Then she continues to shape more cells and lay more eggs.

To fly and hunt, to build more cells and lay more eggs, the queen too needs food. She cannot swallow the mushy food balls she feeds the larvae because her throat is too narrow. A wasp throat is no wider than a paper clip wire. Juices from the food she chews for the larvae give her some nourishment. But she gets her energy mainly from a special sugary fluid that the larvae make from the food the queen has fed them.

The queen must ask the larvae for it. First she drums her antennae rapidly against the edge of a larva's cell. This is a way of inspecting the cell and establishing communication with the larva inside. Then she nibbles the larva's mouthparts. This is the signal. From glands near its mouth, the larva releases its sugary fluid to the queen.

Two weeks after hatching, a larva has grown so big that it completely fills its cell. Yet it manages to twist around and line the cell wall with a thin layer of silk, which it spins from a gland near its mouth. As part of this process, it begins to spin a silk cap over the cell. Around and around the larva goes, layering the silk until the cell is topped by a white dome. The larva has made itself a cocoon.

Throughout the next week, a dramatic transformation takes place. Inside the cocoon, the larva changes from a fat sack with a dark head into something that will look very different. During this silent, hidden period, the changing insect is called a pupa.

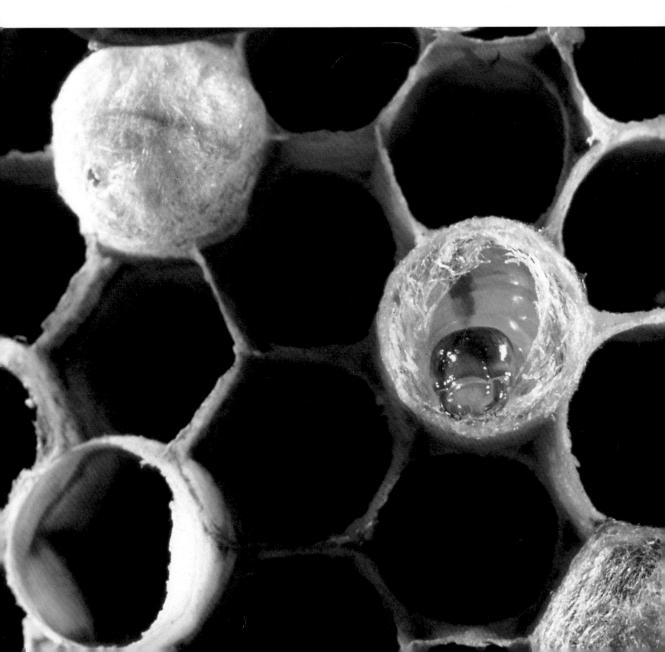

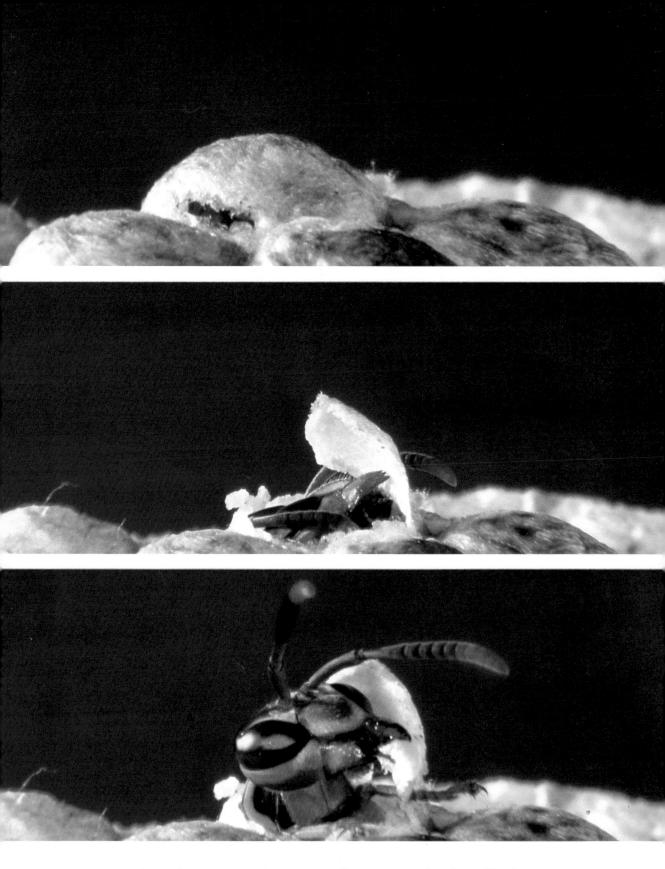

After about a week, a tiny slit appears in the silk dome. Then a larger slit. An adult paper wasp, a worker, is chewing her way free.

Soft and wet, she pushes through the dome and sits quietly while her body dries and hardens. In a social wasp nest, all workers are female.

This worker's well-developed eyes will give her excellent vision for hunting in daylight. And hundreds of receptors on her body will allow her to sense the touches, vibrations, and chemical signals that are part of nest life. It is not known how the chemical signals, called *pheromones*, "travel" throughout the nest. But it is known that the pheromones carry information that triggers different wasp behavior.

The first thing this worker will do is walk to a larva and nibble its mouthparts to receive a drop of sugary liquid for energy. Then she will help the queen with the work of the nest. One of her first jobs will be to chew and soften the food being brought back for the larvae.

These paper wasp workers have just returned to the nest with a piece of a tomato hornworm caterpillar. To kill it they did not sting it; they flew down and bit it with their strong jaws. Then, because it was too heavy to be carried back whole, they pulled it into pieces.

In the nest, workers further tear up the caterpillar and chew the pieces into small, soft food balls for the larvae.

Feeding the larvae is an important task in the life of a social wasp colony. Only larvae that have been well fed make enough sugary fluid to provide energy for all the adults. And well-fed larvae grow up to become healthy workers that care for the nest, catch more food, and feed more larvae.

As more workers hatch, the foundress queen no longer hunts or makes paper. She devotes herself to egg-laying. The workers do everything else, responding to the queen's pheromones and the needs of the colony.

Sometimes workers are thought of as "stunted queens."
They have ovaries for egg-laying, as the queen does. But
because of the way the queen dominates the colony
chemically and physically, workers' ovaries usually remain
undeveloped. If by chance a worker's ovaries do develop
and she begins laying eggs, the queen will probably eat the
eggs. She may even roll and tumble the offending worker
around the nest. A strong queen is also a tyrannical one,
denying reproduction to her worker daughters.

Inside a baldfaced hornet nest, workers are busy feeding their larvae too. One has just returned carrying a piece of a yellowjacket.

Two other workers help chew it into a paste for the hungry larvae. Because a colony of social wasps consumes an enormous quantity of insects, it plays an important role in nature's balance.

On very hot days, it is
the job of some workers to
cool the nest. This one is
vibrating her wings rapidly,
moving air through the nest
like a fan. If the nest remains
too warm, workers go
look for water, which they
bring back and spread over
the combs, especially on the
capped cells, where new
wasps are developing. As
the water evaporates, it
takes heat with it, cooling
the nest.

Workers take turns doing
different jobs in the nest. At
any given time, some may
be out hunting food and
some feeding the larvae.
Others may be cooling the
nest, guarding its entrance,
or cleaning out old cells so
the queen can lay new eggs
in them.

This baldfaced hornet worker is taking care of yet another important job in the nest. She is mixing bits of wood with water, making a papery paste that will become a new layer on the nest's outer sheath. Using her mouth, she rolls the pasty material out and then goes over and over it to make it smooth.

Wasps utilize a wide range of wood pulp, even cardboard on occasion. The paper they make is well adapted for their nest. It is durable and water-resistant, and its layers provide excellent insulation.

Sometime around the middle of summer, baldfaced hornets begin to build extra-large cells near the nest entrance. Because of their placement, the larvae that hatch in these cells tend to be fed first by the workers returning with food. Although larvae further inside the nest may be neglected when this occurs, these large larvae near the entrance need especially good care. In a few weeks they will hatch into queens, distinguished from workers by their larger size. These new queens will mate, find a winter hiding place, then start new nests the following spring.

Here a worker is nibbling the mouthparts of one of the queen larvae, seeking sugary fluid.

About the same time that the new queens are developing, the foundress queen lays eggs that grow into yet another kind of adult wasp. The queen does not fertilize these eggs—she gives them no drops of sperm—so they become neither workers nor queens. They become males. Male wasps do no work in the nest. Their sole purpose in their short life is to mate with the newly hatched queens before winter arrives.

For a while, all three kinds of adults will be emerging: workers, males, and new queens. Then, gradually, a change occurs. As summer turns to autumn, there are fewer caterpillars and other insects to feed to the larvae. So the larvae produce less sugary fluid, and there is less food for the colony. How do the wasps respond to this?

Now the hungry workers do more than nibble the larvae's mouthparts. They bite—hard—all over the larvae, seeking that sweet fluid. The larva at left does not have much fluid to give. It turns away from a biting worker.

Finally, more than biting occurs. The workers hold on with their strong jaws. They yank the larvae out of their cells and pitch them out to die. At first mainly worker larvae are evicted. But as cold weather approaches and food grows scarcer, the remaining queen larvae are at risk of being thrown out. Sometimes workers even gnaw through pupal caps and toss out developing pupae or chew them up for food. The reasons for all this extraordinary behavior are not well understood.

In a paper wasp nest it is the same story. These wasps too are getting rid of their young. Workers remove larvae and sometimes even a pupa, as this photograph shows, and dump them out to die. The behavior of the colony has taken a strange turn. Workers are now participating in the destruction of the nest.

Yet by the time this happens, the foundress queen has achieved her goal. Her colony has been a success. It has produced new queens and males, which have left the nest to mate. And if those fertile queens find good hiding places in which to survive the winter—sometimes clustered together in large groups—life will continue for paper wasps.

In the slanting shadows of an autumn sun, this baldfaced hornet nest hangs abandoned. Most workers have left, never to return. Away from home, they died alone, from cold or hunger or from predation. Most males are also gone. After they mated with new queens, their lives were over. Any wasps that remained have been killed by frost. The foundress queen too has died. Her last larvae and pupae may still be in their cells, never to develop.

But by late summer, a good-sized nest like this probably produced a couple of hundred baldfaced hornet queens, and even more males. A healthy paper wasp nest may have produced several dozen queens and still more males. So there is a good chance that tucked away in an attic or a wall, or deep inside a rotted log or under bark, fertile queens are waiting for spring. When warm weather arrives, they will find some food, scout their surroundings, and set to work on brand new nests. Once again social wasps will be at home.